T0157506

i²

INTENTIONAL   INDEPENDENCE

John Matthew Kilpatrick

BALBOA.
PRESS

A DIVISION OF HAY HOUSE

Balboa Press books may be ordered through booksellers or by contacting:

Balboa Press
A Division of Hay House
1663 Liberty Drive
Bloomington, IN 47403
www.balboapress.com
1 (877) 407-4847

Because of the dynamic nature of the Internet, any web addresses or links contained in this book may have changed since publication and may no longer be valid. The views expressed in this work are solely those of the author and do not necessarily reflect the views of the publisher, and the publisher hereby disclaims any responsibility for them.

The author of this book does not dispense medical advice or prescribe the use of any technique as a form of treatment for physical, emotional, or medical problems without the advice of a physician, either directly or indirectly. The intent of the author is only to offer information of a general nature to help you in your quest for emotional and spiritual well-being. In the event you use any of the information in this book for yourself, which is your constitutional right, the author and the publisher assume no responsibility for your actions.

Scripture quotations taken from the Amplified˙ Bible (AMP), Copyright © 2015 by The Lockman Foundation Used by permission. www.Lockman.org

Any people depicted in stock imagery provided by Thinkstock are models, and such images are being used for illustrative purposes only. Certain stock imagery © Thinkstock.

Print information available on the last page.

ISBN: 978-1-5043-6235-1 (sc)
ISBN: 978-1-5043-6346-4 (e)

Balboa Press rev. date: 07/28/2016

Contents

Chapter 1 1

Chapter 2 15

Chapter 3 29

Chapter 4 47

Chapter 5 59

Greetings and welcome to i²: *Intentional Independence*! I will be your guide through this liberating and life-changing process. We will be taking baby steps through each chapter of i². Take your time and search each level for the things that call out to you, and when you are ready, take the next step.

First, I am sure you're asking: *Why i²? Why intentional independence?* Well, i², the symbol, is a reminder that there are elements and circumstances inside and outside of yourself that you allow to have influence over your decisions and identity. i² is an awareness-raising model. The program allows you to see plainly what is holding you down, and then creates a simple plan to free yourself from these obstacles. i² also serves a reminder that God is calling you closer to Him by calling you to grow into the fullest expression of yourself.

If you see someone with an i² sticker or bracelet, know that they have made a conscious decision to grow into the person they know God intended them to be. i² is hard. Know this first. It takes intention. Empathize with those going through this program, working to live to their fullest potential, and give them a high five while you're at it! They are in a tempering process, and they are there on purpose. They have set a daily reminder to free themselves of the bondage that is offered by the seen and unseen worlds we live in. Simply put; they are remembering how to think for themselves.

In i² Level One we will use the visual of a sailboat to teach you how to harness and direct the situation around you, instead of being a product of it. Once you learn how to sail through life—utilizing the winds of the Holy Spirit and the currents of any-given situation—you can rise above, rather than topple over, and see independence in an entirely new light.

We like this analogy because sails create lift. We like how well the sailboat uses its surrounding environment for its power and rest. Once the art of sailing is mastered, a person can travel anywhere in a sailboat. Anywhere. Sailboats are a completely different craft than any other type of watercraft.

The i² process is going to teach you how to skillfully master your craft, and in doing so, teach you how to navigate the winds and currents of your life with intentionality and awareness. Please allow at least one week per chapter.

Week 1

○   "You" nique: What kind of boat are you on?

Week 2

○   Present and clear: A sound vessel

Week 3

○   Power Prevention: Lifting your anchors

Week 4

    ○   The Shepherd's voice: Raising your sails

Week 5

    ○   As you go: Feel free to move about the harbor

The way we do things is a little different. Think of this as more of a process than a book. Each chapter will have the following five subsections:

1. *The Picture*
2. *The Story*
3. *The Scripture*
4. *The Assignment*
5. *The Application*

The Picture is a visual that helps further explain our point. Following the sailing analogy, these are pictures that serve as reminders of how the process works. Plus, I like pictures. They really are worth 1,000 words.

The Story is a short, personal story of my experience with these concepts, or my experience of seeing these concepts in action. I hope you enjoy reading them as much as I delighted in writing them.

The Scripture. These are simply verses that we drew inspiration from as we wrote the lesson. We use the Amplified Bible in the text, but the King James Version in the research. We hope you enjoy these too. Our intention is that they might even go so far as to inspire you.

The Assignment. This is my favorite section. *The Assignment* will be a small project for you to do upon completion of each chapter. They don't take long, and I promise they don't bite. It's vital to complete each assignment before moving on to the next chapter.

The Application. This is the tough one. You will do something for a week as part of the i² process. We do not ask that you be perfect. We just ask that you get 'er done. These might take all of five minutes out of your day. So say yes. You will be thankful.

Now that you understand the strategy and tactics for working through the i² process, let's take a look at our first two pillars of scripture that are found in the Christian Bible.

Pillar One: "For God did not give us a spirit of timidity or cowardice or fear, but [He has given us a spirit] of power and of love and of sound judgment and personal discipline [abilities that result in a calm, well-balanced mind and self-control]" 2 Timothy 1:7. As I meditated on this scripture, I found it helped me understand more about my personal constitution—who I am and what I'm made of.

In 2 Timothy, Paul answers the question of what we are at our core. Paul says that God gave us a spirit of power, of love, and of sound mind. This is what we are at our core on each of our three levels of existence—mind, body, and spirit. The pressures of life can make you think otherwise, but the pressures of life are just temporary circumstances; they are not at your core.

Let's start by defining each core value. A sound *mind* is one that is completely connected to your heart and the world around you. A sound *mind* is not thrown off course by the changing winds or currents of life. It is present, at peace, and in control of the self.

What is our power? We have the power to alter the status quo of the environment around us. We are constantly, either positively or negatively, impacting our surroundings, whether we intend to or not.

What is love? Well, simply put, love is our energy at its purest and highest form. There is a bright energy that radiates from each of us. It comes from the heart, and is best seen in children—you know, before the world convinces them to cover or shade a portion of this pure light.

Now, I am not going to get into how powerful fear can be, or how inviting it can be to let it into your heart; I am just going to stand firm on the fact that it is not you! It is simply something that can be put on you, but it does not belong to you. Got it?

Have you ever seen light broken into the colors of the rainbow through a prism? It is in this fashion that your spirit gets divided (or branches off) into different parts of you as it enters the world via your heart. The goal is to "Love Hard." To allow for each of the colors of your prism to shine so brightly that the complete and whole white light is maintained as it is translated into the world. Remember: white light is created when all colors combine. Each piece of you that remains hidden, that breaks apart your white light, and, as a result, fragments it into individual colors, limits your ability to love. Take your shades off and love hard!

Our existence on these three levels—mind, body, spirit—is referenced throughout the entire Bible. Not only did God reveal himself on each of these three levels through the Trinity, but Deuteronomy 6:4–5 confirms these three levels of our being, saying, "⁴ Hear, O Israel! The Lord is our God, the Lord is one [the only God]! ⁵ You shall love the Lord your God with all your heart and mind and with all your soul and with all your strength [your entire being]."

The really awesome part of 2 Timothy is that we now have goals for each level of ourselves! We are meant to have a mind that is sound enough to carry the most powerful force in the universe: Love. Through this sound mind, we are to execute God's will in the physical world as His hands and feet. I know that might be a lot to take in. Maybe not, but I will confess it took me about twenty years to fully understand the purpose and design of who and what I am. We are meant to be the light of the world. We are meant to radiate our love under control, positively impacting situations around us. That is what real power is.

Pillar Two: "And do not be conformed to this world [any longer with its superficial values and customs], but be transformed and progressively changed [as you mature spiritually] by the renewing of your mind [focusing on godly values and ethical attitudes], so that you may prove [for yourselves] what the will of God is, that which is good and acceptable and perfect [in His plan and purpose for you]" Romans 12:2.

This scripture affirms for me that this world will try to conform you if you allow it to. If left unacknowledged, this world has the ability to cloud the discernment of God's path for you. It can cause you to forget or to misunderstand what you are really doing here. We will get into this in greater depth in the following chapters. For now, just know that this is the reason for the "intentional" in *Intentional Independence.*

So what about the rest of the verse? What does our friend Paul mean when he says to renew your mind? Is this what George Lucas meant in *Star Wars* when Yoda said: *"You must unlearn what you have learned?"* Well maybe, but I like what Jesus says a little better in Matthew 6:34, "So do not worry about tomorrow; for tomorrow will worry about itself. Each day has enough trouble of its own."

Stay in today! Let the yesterday stay in yesterday. Let tomorrow continue to cook until it is ready for you. Today is where you have your power, and today is what God has prepared for you.

Jesus tells us in Matthew 7:7–8, "⁷Ask and it will be given to you; seek and you will find; knock and the door will be opened to you. ⁸ For everyone who asks receives; the one who seeks finds; and to the one who knocks, the door will be opened."

Seeking is something that no one else can do for you. Seeking is the only prerequisite for taking part in this journey. I promise you, with a seeker's heart and an inquisitive and asking mind that's matched with a knocking hand, you will find things inside and outside of yourself that go far beyond the initial vision of i². All that I ask before we begin this journey is that you do a quick self-analysis and make sure you're entering into this process willing to seek and grow. If we aren't growing, we are dying. Choose growth here and now.

This devotional book is to be paired with a "want to" attitude. We at i² are real people with genuine "want to" attitudes, and we're here to help expose and strengthen all the colors of your spirit. As good as I feel this growth track is, it is not strong enough to overcome a lack of "want to." If growth is not something that you are seeking, i^2 may not be for you.

***

Imagine yourself as a boat. Society wants you to think you need to have the exact same boat as everyone else, and society also believes it needs to be powered by a machine or physical force. Our goal at i^2 is to lessen your dependence on the motor and the rowers and teach you how to sail. We want you to learn to sail not just any boat, we want you to learn how to sail the one-of-a-kind sailboat that is unique to only you. By learning how to sail your vessel, you will be free to go wherever the wind of the Spirit takes you. You will learn the strategies of navigation, and you will experience lift in an entirely new way.

1—You are going to *come to peace* with your boat (you). Comparing to others will only cause you to hide and suppress what makes your boat "you" nique. "You" are as unique as your fingerprint, literally, and "you" were built for a purpose. You are filled with gifts, skills, and a personality that were meant to be used.

2— Right here, right now figure out what your boat can do well, and get good at that. *A sound mind* is present and clear. You see the situation clearly and can easily discern between the pull of the world and the whispers of your heart.

3—You are going to *lift the anchors* up that are currently keeping you from moving when your sails catch wind. You cannot sail freely with anchors still caught up on the ocean floor. Believe me, I have tried.

4—You are going to set sail. Yes, you have spiritual sails and we are going to help you *raise your sails*. In doing so, you will neither need others to row your boat, nor a motor to propel it forward. You will be free to move about your life.

5—Learn how to master your boat. There is a "you" inside that only you and God know. This is the part of you that is "you" nique. It is who He built you to be. This is your destination. Getting there is not going to be measured by the "*whats*" of your life, but rather the "*hows*." A good sailor is not measured by *what* situations he's faced; he's measured by *how* he's handled and navigated through those situations.

I encourage you to pick up the things that ring true to your heart and leave that which does not. Again, what speaks to you, what feels right, what fits who you are as you go through i^2, pick it up and take it with you. The things that don't make your heart ring as we walk together through this process—let those things go.

Chapter 1

The Picture:

A Sailboat—Self Discovery

There are many different ways to power a vessel through water. One of these ways, however, is unlike all the others. This unique way to move a vessel through the water requires a skill that has limitless potential once mastered and is independent of all man made sources of power. This technique to move a vessel through water takes into consideration the surrounding environment and capitalizes on it. This style of moving a vessel through water is navigated by a power that originated from another place and another time. This way, this skill to which I am referring is called sailing.

As the sailor in command of your boat, all you need to move is the surrounding winds and water, and a sound vessel. By listening and responding to your surroundings, you will learn how to harness the power within them.

Before you get onto your boat, let's study it a little. What does it do well? Where are you are going? You are always growing and you are always changing. Let's start making that an intentional process. Do this by setting an inner vision of yourself: *What do I want to look like? Where do I want to go? Who do I want to be?* Imagine what it will feel like to be this inner vision. Imagine what it feels like to be that best you—that "you" that only you and God know about. That is where we are going. You need to set this destination before you set sail. Lastly, take control of the sails, and learn to master your vessel. Now set your course.

The Story

So there I was minding my own business on a random Tuesday night when I got an email that read "SPRC Confidential" in the subject line. I knew this was the governing agency of the Methodist Church of which I have been a member since 1989, so I immediately replied letting the chair know that I had received a confidential email by accident. He kindly replied that I had not received the email by accident; rather, I had been selected by the church to serve on the SPRC (Staff -Parish Relations Committee). If they had known the frustration that I had been experiencing with the church at that time, they would not have ever selected me. This should have been my first indication that God was on the move.

I could hardly wait to get to the first meeting—to make an impact. They selected the right person for the job. Don't worry, church, here I come to save the day!

I arrogantly walked into my first meeting well prepared to unleash the business management skills that I had been carefully sharpening for an opportunity such as this. First things first: I had to get to know these people and their process if I was going to help them. Calmly, I sat down and introduced myself to those that I did not know. There was a noticeable age gap, between me at thirty-three, and everyone else in the room. This might have intimidated most people, but not me. Being a consultant in the world of leadership and business management, I was used to working in an arena where individuals were twice my age or more. Besides, I knew that God's hand was in this situation. He had been before me. What did I have to fear?

Brother Tom opened with a prayer and kicked off the meeting. Brother Tom was a second-generation pastor. This meant that he left a career not in the church to pursue a life of ministry. Brother Tom came from the corporate world. I knew within ten seconds of the meeting that earning his respect would be hard, but if I could do it I would earn the respect of the entire team. He reminded me of a few of the old bulldog type managers that I was consulting for in the business world—very matter of fact, very strong willed. Breaking this bull was going to be fun, or so I thought.

For the most part I really enjoyed the meeting. I contributed with ideas and process solutions, and the group (for the most part), enjoyed my passion and point of view. Something was missing though. As the meeting went on I could not help but think that helping the committee was not the reason God had me in that room.

The reason I was actually there did not hit me until the very end of the meeting. *Your Spiritual Gifts Inventory: From Rediscovering Our Spiritual Gifts* by Charles V. Bryant literally came flying across the table and hit me.

"Here's your copy," Brother Tom, the tosser of the book, said.

"Thanks," I said as I picked it up. "I'll give it a look."

"I would love to know what you score. Why don't you email them to me when you finish? Everyone else got theirs last month."

Was this a challenge? I thought to myself. *Well…challenge accepted.* "Sure will."

After that, Brother Tom prayed us out and the meeting was adjourned.

Anyway, that was the gist of that meeting. I went home, took the test, and did well. I couldn't wait to share my scores with Brother Tom. I was going to blow his mind. Heck, I blew my mind.

I waited a full day before I sent Brother Tom my results. I didn't want to come off too eager to share my high scores. I scored high in Teaching, Exhortation, and Service. I could not wait for him to see what a ready to serve, humble and well-presented teacher I was.

What I got back from him, almost immediately upon emailing my results mind you, was the exact opposite of what I expected. It was a big punch in the gut. It was one sentence: *I look forward to seeing your gifts at work. Luke 12:47–48.*

In case you are wondering, this is what it says:

Luke 12:47–48 says, "[47] And that servant who knew his master's will, and yet did not get ready or act in accord with his will, will be beaten with many lashes [of the whip], [48] but the one who did not know it and did things worthy of a beating, will receive only a few [lashes]. From everyone to whom much has been given, much will be required; and to whom they entrusted much, of him they will ask all the more."

What that told me was that even if he saw the gifts in me, he had not seen them in action. That hurt, but mostly because I knew I was no longer able to hide in the shadows. Brother Tom had called me out Biblically and I was now held accountable. Way to go arrogance…

Honestly, even though I enjoyed serving and teaching, I had never really thought about using those gifts in my life, much less in the church. Well, I could change that. I would jump on the next opportunity to apply one of these gifts, and after that, I'd keep finding opportunities to do more until Brother Tom saw my gifts in action.

I got in the rotation teaching Sunday school. I served with the youth group on trips and Sunday nights. It wasn't long before I started applying my gifts to everything, even my job in consulting. I realized that I liked serving and teaching my clients. I found that as I helped my clients to train their employees and build better businesses they would thank me by buying and recommending my services. The best part was not the increase in revenue that came from a newfound enthusiasm. The best part was that I enjoyed a job that I had previously simply tolerated, just by changing my approach a little.

Up until that point I did not really enjoy consulting. I understood it well enough to be good at it, but I didn't like it.

Here were my secrets to running a successful business:

1. Be intentional and plan
2. Be of value to your end user
3. Manage and define accountability meticulously

If you just do those three things you can take any business or organization a long way. But just because you understand something and you're good at it, doesn't mean you like it. Now I was teaching, presenting, and serving my accounts, and I loved it—all thanks to God, a hard-nosed pastor, and a spiritual gifts test.

I might not have been doing what I loved, but I was doing it in a manner that I loved. Most importantly, I was having fun. I found that using my spiritual gifts in my everyday life changed my paradigm and ignited me. Just the awareness that I could use a particular skillset and potentially enjoy anything that I was doing was liberating.

This experience revealed to me a process—a process of taking what is inside of me and applying it to what is outside of me. Sounds simple, I know, but you and I both know it's not that easy. There are numerous things that can threaten or even prevent this process.

Through intentionality we are going to move past our weaknesses and navigate around our threats. We are going to gain our independence from anything that keeps us from moving when God calls. We want you to take control of your vessel. You, after all, are the one who will be held accountable for it. Next we want you to learn how to completely apply your best self to what is in front of you. In the Introduction this is what we called loving hard. Now go and Love Hard!

The Scripture

1 Corinthians 12:1–31 says, "¹ Now about the spiritual gifts [the special endowments given by the Holy Spirit], brothers and sisters, I do not want you to be uninformed. ² You know that when you were pagans, you were led off after speechless idols; however you were led off [whether by impulse or habit]. ³ Therefore I want you to know that no one speaking by the [power and influence of the] Spirit of God can say, "Jesus be cursed," and no one can say, "Jesus is [my] Lord," except by [the power and influence of] the Holy Spirit.

"4 Now there are [distinctive] varieties of spiritual gifts [special abilities given by the grace and extraordinary power of the Holy Spirit operating in believers], but it is the same Spirit [who grants them and empowers believers]. 5 And there are [distinctive] varieties of ministries and service, but it is the same Lord [who is served]. 6And there are [distinctive] ways of working [to accomplish things], but it is the same God who produces all things in all believers [inspiring, energizing, and empowering them]. 7 But to each one is given the manifestation of the Spirit [the spiritual illumination and the enabling of the Holy Spirit] for the common good. 8 To one is given through the [Holy] Spirit [the power to speak] the message of wisdom, and to another [the power to express] the word of knowledge and understanding according to the same Spirit; 9 to another [wonder-working] faith [is given] by the same [Holy] Spirit, and to another the [extraordinary] gifts of healings by the one Spirit; 10 and to another the working of miracles, and to another prophecy [foretelling the future, speaking a new message from God to the people], and to another discernment of spirits [the ability to distinguish sound, godly doctrine from the deceptive doctrine of man-made religions and cults], to another various kinds of [unknown] tongues, and to another interpretation of tongues. 11 All these things [the gifts, the achievements, the abilities, the empowering] are brought about by one and the same [Holy] Spirit, distributing to each one individually just as He chooses.

"12 For just as the body is one and yet has many parts, and all the parts, though many, form [only] one body, so it is with Christ. 13 For by one [Holy] Spirit we were all baptized into one body, [spiritually transformed—united together] whether Jews or Greeks (Gentiles), slaves or free, and we were all made to drink of one [Holy] Spirit [since the same Holy Spirit fills each life].

"¹⁴ For the [human] body does not consist of one part, but of many [limbs and organs]. ¹⁵ If the foot says, 'Because I am not a hand, I am not a part of the body,' is it not on the contrary still a part of the body? ¹⁶ If the ear says, 'Because I am not an eye, I am not a part of the body,' is it not on the contrary still a part of the body? ¹⁷ If the whole body were an eye, where would the hearing be? If the whole [body] were an ear, where would the sense of smell be? ¹⁸ But now [as things really are], God has placed and arranged the parts in the body, each one of them, just as He willed and saw fit [with the best balance of function]. ¹⁹ If they all were a single organ, where would [the rest of] the body be? ²⁰ But now [as things really are] there are many parts [different limbs and organs], but a single body. ²¹ The eye cannot say to the hand, 'I have no need of you,' nor again the head to the feet, 'I have no need of you.' ²² But quite the contrary, the parts of the body that seem to be weaker are [absolutely] necessary; ²³ and as for those parts of the body which we consider less honorable, these we treat with greater honor; and our less presentable parts are treated with greater modesty, ²⁴ while our more presentable parts do not require it. But God has combined the [whole] body, giving greater honor to that part which lacks it, ²⁵ so that there would be no division or discord in the body [that is, lack of adaptation of the parts to each other], but that the parts may have the same concern for one another. ²⁶ And if one member suffers, all the parts share the suffering; if one member is honored, all rejoice with it.

"²⁷ Now you [collectively] are Christ's body, and individually [you are] members of it [each with his own special purpose and function]. ²⁸ So God has appointed and placed in the church [for His own use]: first apostles [chosen by Christ], second prophets [those who foretell the future, those who speak a new message from God to the people], third teachers, then those who work miracles, then those with the gifts of healings, the helpers, the administrators, and speakers in various kinds of [unknown] tongues. ²⁹ Are all apostles? Are all prophets? Are all teachers? Are all workers of miracles? ³⁰ Do all have gifts of healing? Do all speak with tongues? Do all interpret? ³¹ But earnestly desire and strive for the greater gifts [if acquiring them is going to be your goal].

And yet I will show you a still more excellent way [one of the choicest graces and the highest of them all: unselfish love]."

Matthew 5:13–16 "¹³ You are the salt of the earth; but if the salt has lost its taste (purpose), how can it be made salty? It is no longer good for anything, but to be thrown out and walked on by people [when the walkways are wet and slippery].

"¹⁴ You are the light of [Christ to] the world. A city set on a hill cannot be hidden; ¹⁵ nor does anyone light a lamp and put it under a basket, but on a lampstand, and it gives light to all who are in the house. ¹⁶ Let your light shine before men in such a way that they may see your good deeds and moral excellence, and [recognize and honor and] glorify your Father who is in heaven."

Philippians 2:12–14 "¹² So then, my dear ones, just as you have always obeyed [my instructions with enthusiasm], not only in my presence, but now much more in my absence, continue to work out your salvation [that is, cultivate it, bring it to full effect, actively pursue spiritual maturity] with awe-inspired fear and trembling [using serious caution and critical self-evaluation to avoid anything that might offend God or discredit the name of Christ]. ¹³ For it is [not your strength, but it is] God who is effectively at work in you, both to will and to work [that is, strengthening, energizing, and creating in you the longing and the ability to fulfill your purpose] for His good pleasure.

"¹⁴ Do everything without murmuring or questioning [the providence of God], ¹⁵ so that you may prove yourselves to be blameless and guileless, innocent and uncontaminated, children of God without blemish in the midst of a [morally] crooked and [spiritually] perverted generation, among whom you are seen as bright lights [beacons shining out clearly] in the world [of darkness], ¹⁶ holding out and offering to everyone the word of life, so that in the day of Christ I will have reason to rejoice greatly because I did not run [my race] in vain nor labor without result."

The Assignment:

Spiritual Gifts Test

Your assignment for Chapter 1 is to take a Spiritual Gifts Test. In order to move forward with your assignment for Part 1 you will need at least 3 Gifts from the test that you are confident are buried inside you. It is not important whether you have begun to use your gifts yet, or how developed these gifts are for them to be listed; it only matters that you acknowledge these assets are there.

Personally, I found my hidden gifts by using *Your Spiritual Gifts Inventory From: Rediscovering Our Spiritual Gifts* by Charles V. Bryant. I highly recommend it, as it gave me the awareness and the confidence to start developing my own gifts that God planted inside me. I have also used the online versions from www.SpiritualGiftsTest.com and http://www.umc.org/what-we-believe/spiritual-gifts-online-assessment. They are both equally as awesome.

The Application:

Come to See, Come to Peace

The application for this week is called *Come to....* You are going to *Come to See* an intentional destination as an individual. Then you are going to *Come to Peace* with where you are now in respect to these goals.

First I want you to list 3 Goals for areas of your life that you want to improve upon. Be specific. If it is a position (job or in your personal life), write out that position. If it is your financial status, be specific with your goal. Even if it is not tangible, such as a level of awareness, something that God is calling you to be, or a state of peace—be specific. This is called your *Come to See* list. I want you to be able to see yourself with these goals accomplished. See this new you on the inside, know what it feels like to have attained these goals and be this person. Get to know your goals intimately. Write them down and immediately you will begin to grow toward them.

The next list is *Come to Peace*. You only need to write out exactly where you are in regard to these 3 Goals today. Again, be specific. Come to peace with them. Coming to peace with this starting point does not mean that you have to stay here. If you need help with this, know that there is no amount of anxiety that is going to change where you are. Stop wasting your energy.

Now pull out your monthly calendar. Grab a red and a green marker. Each day mark the day with a red ✗ or a green ✔ depending on whether you moved toward the inner vision of yourself or not. Keep your days isolated. Sometimes bad days can infect good days by stealing your attention. Treat each day as an independent task. Be honest with yourself, and, at the end of the week count your ✗'s and ✔'s. Did you win the week?

Hold onto this list and your calendar. You will use it throughout the entire i² process.

The Questions

1. What is the difference between a spiritual gift and a talent? Why?

2. In Matthew 5, Jesus calls us to be salty (salt of the earth). In what ways are you salty? How?

3. What purpose does a light serve? In what ways are we like a light?

4. If all gifts are from the Spirit are some of them greater than others? Why or why not?

5. Who are spiritual gifts intended for? Why?

Chapter 2

The Picture:

A Sound Vessel

A sound vessel has a proper working sailing system and proper buoyancy just like a sound mind is present and clear. Your mind receives messages about current situations and responds to them. Just as a sailboat receives the winds and currents and harnesses them for power. That's how you make sure you have a properly functioning sailing system. *Is your mind quiet enough to detect the winds of your heart? Are you getting enough sleep? What are your eating habits? Do you get regular exercise? Can you soberly detect the currents of your surrounding situation?* These are all questions that you have to ask yourself. They all have the potential to lower the effectiveness of your vessel, lower the effectiveness of your responses, lowering the impact of yourself. Underneath all the anxiety, grief, jealousy, anger, hurt that your life has added to you, you know you're a sound vessel. Embrace it. That sound version of you is your destination. Small steps forward, day by day, is how we are going to get there.

The Story

Why is it that you can train a dog to do just about anything in the course of an afternoon, but people are so hard to train? Don't think too hard; you might hurt one of the very things that separates us from other animals. That's right, I am talking about your mind. The human mind is a sophisticated bridge that connects what is inside of us at our core, to what is outside of us in the physical world. Your mind controls the process of taking what is seen and making it unseen, as well as taking what is unseen and making it seen. This powerful bridge is best when it is clear, when it is connected, and when it is at peace. This is when your mind is *sound*.

A mind filled by stress can be compared to the conversation on a cell phone that you're trying to have while simultaneously parading in a marching band. What would normally be an easily understood exchange of words under "normal" circumstances, quickly becomes difficult to hear. It becomes a convoluted utterance of unintelligable sounds clanking around among musical notes. It might not even sound like words, more like noises banging together without rhyme or reason. That's your brain on stress.

On the other hand, a mind that is in a state of receiving or waiting, quietly in a state of peace, can be likened to having that same conversation, but now you're sitting quietly by a gently flowing brook on a warm day. This quiet place of stillness is the goal—the everyday goal.

Now ask yourself these questions. *Where is your mind? Is it here, now? Is your mind noisy and crowded? Do you find it peaceful and content?* It is good practice to be conscious of the noise that echoes in your head. These echoes have great impact on your outlook and perception of life. Your mind has the potential to be a runaway boat if you do not assume the role of the captain. Once in motion this boat can become very difficult to stop. After all, sailboats don't have brakes.

This story is ultimately about me trying to get my mind under control. It began with meditation. I didn't understand the discipline needed for meditation when I first tried it. I was in college, and my brother, Chris, was in town on leave from the Marines. I was talking with him about how noisy my mind had become. I told him that between work, school, and a small attempt at a personal life, I couldn't keep it quiet.

Long story short, he told me that if I couldn't gain control of my mind, I'd never have a chance at gaining control of situations in my life. I would always just be a product of whatever situation I was in. Like a pinball reactively bouncing its way from barrier to barrier, I would be doing the same in the game of life. This sounded horrible! I wanted no part of this pinball lifestyle, so I set out to learn how to meditate. I was committed, I was determined to learn self-control, but I had no idea what I was doing.

By the time he returned on his next leave, I had nothing good to report. My mind only seemed to speed up as I tried to clear it. This is when he shared the secret of Meditation Momentum. He told me to start by controlling my actions. Once I could control myself physically, then I should work on controlling myself mentally. Trying to jump straight into controlling my mind was too big of a task for me to take on. I needed to build momentum.

"m^2" was born. When I started m^2, I could hardly sit still for five minutes. Now, stillness is my vice! Meditation Momentum gave me a step one—something to master before having to go all in.

I will tell you what I found out. My brother gave me a pretty good plan, and I have given it to you as *The Application* section of this chapter. I hope that it works as well as it did for me. After a few weeks of building Meditation Momentum, I was able to identify the difference between the noise that echoed in my mind from the world around me and the soft whispers of my heart. Still a long way to go for a "sound mind," but it was a start. I was at least able to discern what was coming from where. Most importantly, no matter what was bouncing around my head, I had control of my actions. I learned self-control.

Coming to peace with all of the noise running around in my head was only part of the job; I still had to figure out a way to quiet it. I had to get to the source of where these thoughts were originating. I knew I was naturally anxious about the next day or next step in my life. That had been a constant. If that were not enough, I was flooded with grief from a few big mistakes in my past. Needless to say, my attention was somewhere else. If my mind were an attention pie, by the time it got around the table to the present moment, there'd be none left!

In Matthew 6:34, Jesus says, "So do not worry about tomorrow; for tomorrow will worry about itself. Each day has enough trouble of its own."

When I found out that the Jewish day ended at sundown, this verse really made a lot more sense to me. I actually began a specific style of prayer for sundown that helped me to stay in the day. Every night at sundown I ended my day. I'd say a prayer of thanksgiving for the day that is now behind me. Then I'd pray for forgiveness for the situations that I did not handle in the manner I knew I could have.

Finally, I conceded to do my very best, daily, to show the Lord my heart; my own selfish desires. Acting like I did not have personal desires just caused me to hide part of myself from God. God knows you better than you know yourself. He built you. Instead of acting like I didn't have part of myself shadowed, instead of acting as if a selfish will of my own did not exist, I restructured. I found that prioritizing

His will for me first, and my own second, was a much more effective and efficient strategy.

After the sunset each day now, I do my best to be honest with Him. Hoping that He can find a way to weave my own selfish will into His will for me. Then my day is done, never to return. Praying this prayer at sundown made going to bed in peace a reality. Then when I wake up I am starting a brand new day. It is white as snow!

Letting God see all of your heart, all of your hope, all of your desires, allows the mind and body to rest while He works. The next day you wake up knowing His signature will be on situations that come your way. This changes the way you look at your day. It changed the way I looked at my life! I just took it one day at a time. You do this and you will begin to expect great things!

This prayer at sundown helped me take a big step towards being present, but I still had work to do. Little ideas still take my attention away from the present moment and move me into my imagination—into the anxiety of the future and the regret of the past.

For this ongoing issue, I had to learn a little bit about how the brain works, and I am glad that I did. You see, your mind fires between two points. You have a sender and a receiver. The first time it fires between two points it is a fresh connection. The longer and more often you send and receive between two points, the deeper the channel gets in that direction. This will not be on the assignment, I promise—I just want you to have some insight because it will play into your understanding of how I came up with a strategy of disposing unwanted thoughts.

The best way I've found to rid my head of thoughts that would not simply fade away was to write them down, study them briefly, and then pray about them. Seeing the thoughts in front of me helped put them into perspective, not to mention it took them "out" of my head; they were no longer constantly firing and digging deeper. Writing things down is not *The Application* in this chapter, but I do highly recommend it.

After taking on these two practices of m^2—praying at sunset and writing down random, unwanted thoughts—I really got a clear idea of why God created us to have a sound mind. Our minds are drawbridges that connect the physical world to the spiritual one. Like any drawbridge, it has the ability to break the connection with the other side. No matter where you find yourself, work to keep the connection sound.

God will send into your life no more than what the foundation of the bridge will support. If you want to increase what God is sending across your bridge, strengthen the foundation. Discipline your mind and gain control of your bridge.

You and only you get to decide what moves from the physical world, through your mind, and into your heart. You also are the one who gives permission to what is allowed to move from inside you into the outside, physical world. That is a pretty big responsibility. Take it seriously.

You have to build a mind sound enough to see the best you on the inside; the "You"nique you. This vision will be our destination when we eventually set sail. Where you are right now will be our starting point. When plotting a course an accurate starting point is every bit as valuable as a specific destination.

Let go of control, let go of everything that is outside of the present moment and rest in the arms of God. Once this is accomplished, lean into your feelings; do not run from them. It is through peace and acceptance of you and your situation that you are able to get on the boat. And intentionally wanting to get on your boat is the first step in moving toward your destination: the best you.

The Serenity Prayer

God grant me the serenity
to accept the things I cannot change;
the courage to change the things I can;
and wisdom to know the difference.

—*Reinhold Niebuhr*

The Scripture

1 Corinthians 7:17–24 "[17] Only, let each one live the life which the Lord has assigned him, and to which God has called him [for each person is unique and is accountable for his choices and conduct, let him walk in this way]. This is the rule I make in all the churches. [18] Was anyone at the time of his calling [from God already] circumcised? He is not to become uncircumcised. Has anyone been called while uncircumcised? He is not to be circumcised. [19] Circumcision is nothing, and uncircumcision is nothing, but what matters is keeping the commandments of God. [20] Each one should

remain in the condition in which he was [when he was] called.

"²¹ Were you a slave when you were called? Do not worry about that [since your status as a believer is equal to that of a freeborn believer]; but if you are able to gain your freedom, do that. ²² For he who was a slave when he was called in the Lord is a freedman of the Lord, likewise he who was free when he was called is a slave of Christ. ²³ You were bought with a price [a precious price paid by Christ]; do not become slaves to men [but to Christ]. ²⁴ Brothers, let each one remain with God in that condition in which he was [when he was] called."

Romans 12:1-5 "¹ Therefore I urge you, brothers and sisters, by the mercies of God, to present your bodies [dedicating all of yourselves, set apart] as a living sacrifice, holy and well-pleasing to God, which is your rational (logical, intelligent) act of worship. ² And do not be conformed to this world [any longer with its superficial values and customs], but be transformed and progressively changed [as you mature spiritually] by the renewing of your mind [focusing on godly values and ethical attitudes], so that you may prove [for yourselves] what the will of God is, that which is good and acceptable and perfect [in His plan and purpose for you].

"³ For by the grace [of God] given to me I say to everyone of you not to think more highly of himself [and of his importance and ability] than he ought to think; but to think so as to have sound judgment, as God has apportioned to each a degree of faith [and a purpose designed for service]. ⁴ For just as in one [physical] body we have many parts, and these parts do not all have the same function or special use, ⁵ so we, who are many, are [nevertheless just] one body in Christ, and individually [we are] parts one of another [mutually dependent on each other]."

Matthew 7:1-3 "¹Do not judge *and* criticize *and* condemn [others unfairly with an attitude of self-righteous superiority as though assuming the office of a judge], so that you will not be judged [unfairly]. ² For just as you [hypocritically] judge others [when you are sinful and unrepentant], so will you be judged; and in accordance with your standard of measure [used to pass out judgment], judgment will be measured to you. ³ Why do you look at the [insignificant] speck that is in your brother's eye, but do not notice *and* acknowledge the [egregious] log that is in your own eye?

The Assignment:

Let Go and Let God

When you judge someone you essentially challenge whatever that person is battling and say to it "bring it on." I don't know about you, but I don't have time to go around looking for fights, especially ones that I am not confident I can win. Situational judgment moves you off the mark—the mark being "here." It says to your heart that you should be somewhere else; or worse, it says you should be somebody else. This is another trap, and will only weaken your ability to navigate the current situation.

Mastering your thoughts does not mean that you have complete control over thoughts that randomly pop into your mind; after all, Jesus himself was tempted by Satan. The point of control comes when you decide if you are going to attach to the thought by giving it attention which will eventually turn into action, or if you are going to let it pass through your mind like a rumbling cloud in the sky. Jesus told Satan to "get behind" Him. I recommend you do the same.

To do this let's master the art and skill of letting go. I want you to call out a quick list of all the things that rival for your attention. Then pray over them and give them to God.

- *What has you anxious about tomorrow? PRAY. Now give it to God.*

- *What can you not let go of from yesterday? PRAY. Now give it to God.*

- *What has you wanting to be somewhere else? PRAY. Now give it to God.*

- *What judgment are you now facing? PRAY. Now give it to God.*

The answers to these questions are the traps by which your mind has been bound. Shame keeps your attention in the past. Fear moves it into the future. These forces pull your attention off the mark that is the present moment.

The Application:

Five Minutes of Stillness Every Day for a Week

Before you learn to control your thoughts, learn to control yourself. Set a timer and sit completely still for five minutes. Do not worry with trying to quiet your mind until you learn to quiet yourself. The first day the timer will seem like it will never go off. Then within a couple of days, you will be wishing for more time. Do this once a day with your eyes closed. Again, don't worry about what your mind does, yet. Mark on your calendar ✔'s for days when you take five and ✗'s for the days when you do not.

New Prayer Schedule—I want you to consider a humble morning prayer and a holy evening prayer into your daily routine.

Humble Morning Prayer

Dear Heavenly Father,

Thank you for the day that you have made for me. Please show me the path that you have laid for me through it. Guide and direct me down it. Send me the wisdom, the peace, the patience and the love to do as you would have me. Thank you for your grace as I am sure that I will miss your mark. I pray that with your help I make the best of your will for this day.

In Christ's name,
Amen

Holy Evening Prayer

Dear Heavenly Father,

Thank you for this day and all of the situations of it. Forgive me where I mishandled the situations that you sent me. I pray that your timeless mercy and grace cover my misses. I pray now that you see my heart as you build my tomorrow. I will hide no desire or want from you as I pray that you are able to harmonize my heart with your melody for me. I will now rest while you work Lord. I pray that when I wake I will seek out you and your signature on the day that you have made for me.

In Christ's name,
Amen

The Questions

1. How do you stay within the day and still have a plan for life?

2. What are some things or situations that pull you out of the moment and why?

3. How do you stop judgment at its core?

4. Is there a difference between meditation and prayer? If so, what is it?

5. What are some reasons that it is good to be here and now? Why?

Chapter 3

The Picture:

Lifting Your Anchors

Face it, there are things that are weighing you down. There are things in your life that keep you from moving when God calls. You cannot begin to go anywhere until you lift your anchor; or in some cases, anchors. The first step in lifting your anchor is to acknowledge it. Calling your anchor out will get it off the ground and allow for you to get moving. However, it is important to know that although you can still get moving if your anchor is off the ground it will add stress to the vessel. You are at your best when your anchor(s) are lifted completely out of the water.

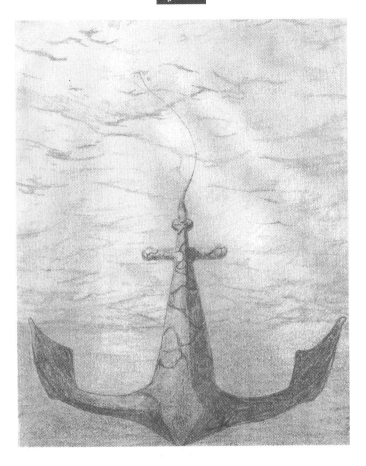

The Story

Now that you are on your "you" nique boat (step one), the next step is to lift your anchors so that you can move when your sails are filled with wind. If your anchors are still on the ground when you raise your sails, you will only add stress to the boat itself—not to mention you won't go anywhere.

Again, you don't have to have the anchors all the way up to move. So don't let perfection prevent improvement.

What are your anchors? I wish I could answer that for you. I know that calling out my own anchors and keeping them up is my *other* fulltime job. That is a big part of how this whole thing works. Me minding my own ship is the best thing that I can do for you. If my vessel is sound, my anchors are up, and my sails are high, I can move when the wind of the Holy Spirit blows. You are the only one who can truly intentionally lift your anchors. This is *your* other fulltime job.

Resist the urge to shift your attention to anyone else's boat or anyone else's anchors. This will only make lifting your own anchors more difficult. We are going to take a look at some of the most common anchors this world offers. I am talking about debt, habits or addictions, society and your inner circle.

Debt. The Bible is very specific about the warnings of debt and how it can weigh us down. The Bible also lays out a 7-year plan for debt. This 7-year reactive debt plan is a great way to get you back to square one.

The credit system wants you to seek treatment, but not a cure. There must be a plan of action to remove it. Think about this; if you carry a credit balance month-to-month you are lessening your future disposable income. If a guarantee to have less money in the future doesn't get you motivated, then how about this; debt alone has the ability to prevent you from moving when God calls. It will keep you in a situation that you know is wrong, ultimately keeping you from your independence.

I know what you are thinking: *I just need to make more money.* Yes, increasing your income will increase your disposable income; but know this, if you do not build disciplined money-management practices with a little bit of money, by the time you make more money, these bad money habits will only be more exemplified and the consequences will be more severe. Be thankful that you get the opportunity to learn how to manage your money before your bank account expands.

The 7-year debt-free plan:

- Take everything you owe and divide it into monthly payments over the next seven years.
- Stop buying things that you do not need. A want vs. needs list helps with this.
- Put a cap on what you allow yourself to spend impulsively.

After dividing your debt over 7 years, the second part of the strategy to paying off your debt is to minimize your living expenses. I know, that tastes like vinegar. But trust me when I tell you this is not a lifetime treatment—this is the cure. Do it. For 7 years make decisions for which you will be thankful for the rest of your life. Trust me; investing in the "tomorrow you" is the best thing you can do.

Before my wife and I started the 7-year debt-free plan, we were paying out the equivalent of a mortgage payment in student loans, credit cards, and car payments, and we were going nowhere. God could have been knocking on our door and we wouldn't have noticed. We were way too busy chasing payments. I had a job that was paying me very well but was having negative impacts on my health and my family. Plus, I knew it was not where I was supposed to be. Even though I was fortunate enough to be successful in my career, I could not run from the fact that I was not doing what God was asking. I was stuck. This static state affected everything in our lives, including debt management.

I could not get out of my current situation until I lessened my dependence on money. Eliminating our debt was how we were going to do this. And that is just what we did. We simplified our lives and attacked each credit line independently. We chose the debt with the heaviest anchors (interest rates) and removed them first. One-by-one, we removed payments from our disposable income. The net gain became, over time, the equivalent of a healthy raise, bringing more disposable income into the family as we were paying off our debt. This is because we had prioritized with steps two and three of the plan, and so we were living smarter.

This little bit of extra cash helped us to build momentum. We were able to get continuously more aggressive with our 7-year plan. Before we knew it, aside from our mortgage (which I will get to in a minute), we were debt free, and we had increased our disposable income by $3,500 per month!

That was the same cash value as $50,000 in salaried income. This move alone made it possible for me to walk away from my "golden handcuffs." It gave me the freedom to start my own company. Even though I made just about $50,000 less than I was making as a sales manager that first year, we took no hit in our disposable income due to God's help, a faithful wife and the 7-year debt plan. We had lifted the anchor of debt. It always amazes me what help God will provide when you start moving towards Him.

Recap:

1. Tally up all your debt.
2. Determine "what" from your monthly expenses is not required for your house to function, and minimize expenses you're not willing to completely eliminate.
3. Take the total of the monthly cuts you've made and add that to the payment of your debt that has the highest interest rate.
4. Pay your debts off by paying the minimum on all but the one you're adding your new disposable income to.
5. As you pay off the greatest debt, add the total amount that you were paying to that bill to the next debt in line.
6. Repeat Step 5, and so on. As you cross the bills off the list, you will naturally resist the urge to spend the extra money until all debts are gone, because this system is so motivating to witness in action.
7. After you've paid your last debt, move this extra money to your mortgage…until it is gone.

Here is a loose and conservative hypothetical 7-year plan (because you know I like visuals):

Total Debt = $230,000

- 4% APR Mortgage = $150,000 ($1,500/mo.)
- 4% APR Student Loans = $25,000 ($1,000/mo.)
- Credit Cards = $20,000 ($1,000/mo. total)
  - 22% APR Main CC = $15,000 ($500/mo.)
  - 27% APR Department A CC = $1,000 ($100/mo.)
  - 27% APR Department B CC = $1,500 ($150/mo.)
  - 27% APR Department C CC = $1,500 ($150/mo.)
  - 19% Gas CC = $1,000 ($100/mo.)
- 5% APR Car #1 = $20,000 ($450/mo.)
- 5% APR Car #2 = $15,000 ($350/mo.)

Monthly cuts with zero credit card usage = +$200
Total monthly debt payments = $4,300

Now—

1. Stop using your credit cards
2. Take the total of the all debt except your mortgage and divided by 7 years. Then take that total and divide it over 12 months.
   a. $80,000/7 = $11,429 per year
   b. $11,429 /12 = $953 per month—this is the extra amount per month needed to be applied to your debt.

c. Obtaining $953 in cash to apply to my debt is my first goal.

3. Intentionally attack the lowest balance with the highest interest rate.

    a. a. With my $200 found in the household cuts added to the minimum payment, I am able to payoff Department A Credit Card in five months.

4. Now that's gone, so add that $100 from the minimum payment of that credit card to the $200.

    a. New value of your extra monthly cash after five months = $300

5. Intentionally attack the lowest balance with the highest interest rate.

    a. With the $300 you are able to pay off the balance of Department B Credit Card in five months.

6. Add that $150 from the minimum payment to the $300

    a. New total for available extra cash after ten months = $450

7. Intentionally attack the lowest balance with the highest interest rate.

    a. With the $450 you are able to pay off the balance of Department C Credit Card in four months.

8. Add that $150 from the minimum payment to the $450

    a. New total for available extra cash after one year and two months = $600

9. Intentionally attack the lowest balance with the highest interest rate.
    a. With the new total of $600/mo. available, you are able to pay of the balance of the Gas Card in 2 months.
10. Add that $100 from the minimum payment to the $600.
    a. New total for extra cash available after one year and four months = $700
11. Intentionally attack the lowest balance with the highest interest rate.
    a. With the $700 you have available now, you are able to pay of the balance of the Main Card in one year and ten months.
12. Add that $500 from the minimum payment to the $700
    a. New total after three years and two months = $1,200
    b. First goal reached! Congratulations!

Reassess your debt—

Total debt = $170,500

- Mortgage = $130,000 ($1,500/mo.)
- 4% APR Student loans = $21,000 ($800/mo.)
- Credit Cards = $0
- 5% APR Car = $12,000 ($450/mo.)
- 5% APR Car = $7,500 ($350/mo.)

New total for monthly debt = $3,100

13. Intentionally attack the lowest balance with the highest interest rate.
    a. With the $1,200 you are able to pay of the balance of Car #2 in 7 months.
14. Add that $350 from the minimum payment to the $1,200.
    a. New total after three years and nine months = $1,550
15. Intentionally attack the lowest balance with the highest interest rate.
    a. With the $1,550 you are able to pay of the balance of Car #2 in 8 months.
16. Add that $450 from the minimum payment to the $1,550.
    a. New total after four years and five months = $2,000
17. Intentionally attack the lowest balance with the highest interest rate.
    a. With the $2,000 you are able to pay of the balance of the student loan in 11 months with.
18. Add that $800 from the minimum payment to the $2,000.
    a. New total after five years and four months = $2,800

Now we still have almost 2 years left and you have given yourself a $2,800 cash raise per month, which is the equivalent of $48,000 annual raise in salary in a 30% tax bracket. Nice work! It only took you five years and four months! I never said the 7-year plan was perfect….

Now let's move to Phase 2 to the proactive debt plan— your mortgage.

The goal is to build equity after you have plugged all of your holes. You still have some debt left so lets look at it:

Total debt—

○ 4% APR Mortgage = $130,000

Total payments—

○ 4% APR Mortgage = $1,500 with only 50% going to principle

1. Add your $2,800 to the $1,500 for a total payment of $4,300 per month.
   a. $3,550 applied to principal per month
   b. Your mortgage will be paid off in 37 months

New total after eight years and three months = $4,300. This is a $74,000 raise equivalent in salaried income in the 30% tax bracket. You now have $150,000 in equity and 0 debt. Buy a new house financing no more than $100,000 over 7 years and your house payment will not exceed $1,600 for as many times as you want to repeat this process. If you were to repeat this cycle until you caught up with the 15-year new aggressive mortgage term, at the end of 15 years with the 7-year plan, you will have $230,000 in equity and be debt free vs. the $150,000 that you would have on the 15-year "aggressive" bank plan.

One more scenario for those of you who are fortunate enough to get your hands on the proactive debt plan before you have accrued any debt of substance.

○ Budget for a house payment of $1,700
○ Finance $100,000 on your first house
○ At $1,700 per month it will be paid off in 7 years

Repeat two times and in 21 years from day one you will be in your third house with $300,000 in equity and no debt. If you start when you are twenty-two, by the time you're forty-three you will be without a mortgage payment and in a $300,000 house. Ask any forty-three-year-old if they wish they had done this when they were twenty-two, and their answer will be yes. Comparing this to a 30-year mortgage in the same $300,000 with payments being equal at $1,700/ mo.—at forty-three you are still roughly around $175,000 in debt with only $125,000 in equity.

***

So, what about some of the other anchors?

What about addictions?
What about your inner circle?
What about fear?

First, let's not look at just the addictions that your society labels as bad. Let's look at anything that has control over you. I want you to call out anything that has the potential to keep you from moving toward the best you. This is anything that you have built into your daily practice that has the potential to control you. This "anchor," whether you like it or not, is something that you serve. This can be drugs and narcotics, of course, but this can also be poor eating habits, poor health habits, and even poor work habits. If you are not sure what else is weighing you down and keeping you from moving, ask God to show you. Believe me, He will; you just need to be willing to accept His answer.

Anchors can be people or even pressures that society puts on you. We all have something, some weakness, which we must overcome. Everyone has something that threatens his or her self-control. Keep your eyes on your own paper! Any attention paid to other people's anchors will keep you from effectively and efficiently removing your own. Lifting your anchor is part of the growth process. Being able to lift your own anchor is the barrier to entry for sailing your vessel.

When you figure your anchors out, write them down. You must call them out. Then hold yourself accountable for keeping them off the ground. It is best to get your anchors out of the water and locked into place; however, calling them out and getting them off the ground is your task for now. Only compare yourself to the "you" of yesterday. Don't waste any time concerning yourself with the anchors of others unless you're looking for a new strategy, or they've asked you for help. Otherwise, it's a waste of time and will not help you to get moving.

The Scripture

Proverbs 22:7 says, "The rich rules over the poor, And the borrower is servant to the lender."

Deuteronomy 15:1–5 says, "[1] At the end of every seven years you shall grant a release (remission, pardon) from debt. [2] This is the regulation for the release: every creditor shall forgive what he has loaned to his neighbor; he shall not require repayment from his neighbor and his brother, because the Lord's release has been proclaimed. [3] You may require repayment from a foreigner, but whatever of yours is with your brother [Israelite] your hand shall release. [4] However, there will be no poor among you, since the Lord will most certainly bless you in the land which the Lord your God is giving you as an inheritance to possess, [5] if only you will listen to and obey the voice of the Lord your God, to observe carefully all these commandments which I am commanding you today. [6] When the Lord your God blesses you as He has promised you, then you will lend to many nations, but you will not borrow; and you will rule over many nations, but they will not rule over you."

Matthew 6: 19–33 "[19] Do not store up for yourselves [material] treasures on earth, where moth and rust destroy, and where thieves break in and steal. [20] But store up for yourselves treasures in heaven, where neither moth nor rust destroys, and where thieves do not break in and steal; [21] for where your treasure is, there your heart [your wishes, your desires; that on which your life centers] will be also.

"[22] The eye is the lamp of the body; so if your eye is clear [spiritually perceptive], your whole body will be full of light [benefiting from God's precepts]. [23] But if your eye is bad [spiritually blind], your whole body will be full of darkness [devoid of God's precepts]. So if the [very] light inside you [your inner self, your heart, your conscience] is darkness, how great and terrible is that darkness!

"24 No one can serve two masters; for either he will hate the one and love the other, or he will be devoted to the one and despise the other. You cannot serve God and mammon [money, possessions, fame, status, or whatever is valued more than the Lord].

"25 Therefore I tell you, stop being worried or anxious (perpetually uneasy, distracted) about your life, as to what you will eat or what you will drink; nor about your body, as to what you will wear. Is life not more than food, and the body more than clothing? 26 Look at the birds of the air; they neither sow [seed] nor reap [the harvest] nor gather [the crops] into barns, and yet your heavenly Father keeps feeding them. Are you not worth much more than they? 27 And who of you by worrying can add one hour to [the length of] his life? 28 And why are you worried about clothes? See how the lilies and wildflowers of the field grow; they do not labor nor do they spin [wool to make clothing], 29 yet I say to you that not even Solomon in all his glory and splendor dressed himself like one of these. 30 But if God so clothes the grass of the field, which is alive and green today and tomorrow is [cut and] thrown [as fuel] into the furnace, will He not much more clothe you? You of little faith! 31 Therefore do not worry or be anxious (perpetually uneasy, distracted), saying, 'What are we going to eat?' or 'What are we going to drink?' or 'What are we going to wear?' 32 For the [pagan] Gentiles eagerly seek all these things; [but do not worry,] for your heavenly Father knows that you need them. [33] But first and most importantly seek (aim at, strive after) His kingdom and His righteousness [His way of doing and being right—the attitude and character of God], and all these things will be given to you also."

The Assignment

Calling out Your Anchors

So, what about some of the other anchors? What about addictions? What about bad habits? Let's look at anything that has control over you. This includes but is not limited to: sugar, caffeine, television, social media, gossip, drugs, food, people, etc. I want you to look at anything that has the potential to keep you from moving toward your destination: the best you. If you are not sure what else is weighing you down, ask God to show you, and just be willing to accept His answer.

When you have identified your anchors, write these down and call them out. Use these anchors to create an accountability calendar.

My anchors keeping me from setting sail under the power of the winds of the Holy Spirit:

1. _____

2. _____

3. _____

4. _____

5. _____

The Application

Anchor Accountability

a^2

Pull out your calendar from week one. You are going to measure the wins and losses of each day by whether or not these specific anchors have prevented you from moving toward the best you. Compare only to the "you" of the previous day by asking yourself: *Did I move forward or did I just tug on my anchor?*

Use a green marker for a ✔ on the calendar for your positive days, and a red ✗ for everything else. This is important! Begin and end your days with a ✔ or an ✗! Do not mix them. Focus only on one day at a time and then at the end of the week, tally your wins and losses.

The Questions

1. In what ways do you serve your anchors? Can your anchors serve you?

2. What is the difference between having your anchor off the ground and having it all the way up?

3. Who can help you lift your anchors?

4. Can you see yourself debt free in seven years? What does it feel like?

5. When can it be a good thing to have an anchor? Why?

Chapter 4

The Picture:

Lifting Your Sails

It is time for you to lift your sails. Lift your sails as high as your sound mind will take them. Stand upright and become sensitive to what is going on in your heart. Be attentive to what the current situation is telling you because your situation is the water that you must sail through. This will require you to be vulnerable enough to let your surrounding environment impact you. *Is the water peaceful and calm? Are there undercurrents?* Once you have a read on the situation, return to center and find the wind of God's will for you within it. What would He want you to do? Let it lift you up, propelling you toward your destination: the best you. When you find yourself in a position to use one of your spiritual gifts for the benefit of someone else, take it! It will fill your sails and provide life, ultimately lifting and moving you.

The Story

A few years ago my wife and I purchased some property. It was just over 6 acres; not a ton of land, but just enough to where you could get lost on it if you really tried. The land had gone untouched for about twenty years. Prior to that it had been cleared of all but a few large trees. So, for roughly twenty years this piece of land had been a free-for-all for growth. Here is an i^2 Level 2 note: When conditions are prime, growth happens.

I could not wait for the papers to be signed, so I could start blazing trails on the property. Conventional wisdom (and my wife) would tell you to simply hire a professional, or, at the least, rent some heavy machinery to come and knock down what we referred to as our Alabama jungle.

Too bad I've never been one to follow conventional wisdom, especially when I had a brand new machete and hatchet that I just knew would be perfect for the job.

Here is what I learned:

1. 6.5 acres of Alabama jungle is a lot to clear by hand.
2. Successfully removing yourself from a green briar patch or blackberry patch is a delicate situation, not something that is accomplished with force.

You could have probably guessed about my first lesson, but the second, well, I hope by listing it, that I will save you from that ever occurring. I cannot tell you how many times I tried to use force to get myself "unstuck" from the thorns that would attack me as I was trying to make a path in the woods. And yes, they did attack me. One little thorn would grab my shirt or pant leg and before I could control the instinctual "jerk," the entire bush would jump out of the woods and ensnare me. The harder I fought, the deeper the thorns went into my skin. With every move more thorns would leap out of the woods like they had magic powers and latch on.

After about a year of donating blood to the woods, and not a whole lot of land clearing to show for it, I figured I needed a new strategy. So I invited my brother, Chris the Marine, to come and walk the property with me. Chris is a woodsman and has been for as long as I can remember. You will get to know him and his Society of the Wild in Level 3 of i². For now, let me just say that he is the type of person who can take off walking, be gone for a few weeks, and actually look healthier—revived—when he returns. He calls it a "walkabout." I asked him to come "walkabout" with me in my Alabama jungle.

What I witnessed was humbling. Instead of fighting through the brush like I had, Chris would carefully, peacefully, and with little to no protection on his legs and feet, move through the brush unscathed. Each time a thorn would jump out and grab him, instead of freaking out (like I had), he would simply stop, remove the single briar, and continue on his way.

Hmm…? Was this peaceful approach to removing the literal "thorn in my side" a better approach than my flailing and aggressive swinging machete? Was this calm and deliberate technique for moving through the forest less painful than my out of control combative approach? You bet it was. Was it faster, too? Yep.

You see, I thought control meant showing the woods that I was the boss. I thought control meant imposing my will upon the thorns that were causing me so much grief. I thought wrong. Control is actually acknowledging the traps and thorns and maintaining a level of peace and patience as I free myself of them. Control was not giving the briars any more attention than they deserved. I learned that by keeping my sights on my next best move, and not getting lost in the "fight" with the forest, I was free to move with the forest, not against it. This was real control. This was self-control.

The woods were only fighting me because I fought them first. They were fighting back. This was an important lesson for me. Our property was not the only arena where I was rampaging with my machete. My tact for life mirrored my tact for the woods. I would use all of my physical ability to motor my will through my life. It hurt. It was literally me against the world. Now don't get me wrong, I was winning—so long as you count winning as high blood pressure, eighty-hour workweeks, and a house that was over run with grief and anxiety. So, yes, it is possible, you can motor your way through life. But at what cost?

I had to learn a new way. I had to learn to trust in something bigger than myself. That was hard. Waiting and listening was not a strategy that was easily adopted.

1. I had to trust that God was sending me exactly what I needed to move my life forward in the direction that He intended it to go.
2. I had to trust that this new direction was what would be best for my family and me.
3. I had to let go of my will, focus solely on handling the situations that I was faced with, and face them using excellence without reservation.

Once I learned to walk in a non-combative manner, I was able to receive all that a situation had for me. I learned how to wait and listen. I learned how to stop and be still. This is how you begin to understand why the situations that you face are in front of you in the first place. This is how you begin to understand how to use them to get to your final destination: the best you.

There is a big difference between receiving and projecting. Receiving is sailing—taking full advantage of what is happening around you to pull you toward your goal. Projecting is taking matters into your own hands. It is a battle of wills, so to speak. You can accept His will for you, or project your own. Those are your only choices.

Listen! God is trying to speak to you. He wishes to speak through you. He is trying to put you in situations that help to unfold and expand the "you" that is wrapped up and bound inside of you. The trouble is you cannot begin to understand what is happening inside of your heart, as long there is so much noise in your mind. You cannot hear it.

Your heart is where true thought comes from, original thought, divinely inspired and pure. It is where the Good Shepherd speaks to you in a lowly and peaceful voice. Know the difference between the echoes of your mind and the whispers of your heart. Go deeper and beyond your five physical senses and learn a new language—the language of your heart.

We will refine this process throughout the different levels of i^2, but for now just know that you need to be sensitive to what is happening in your heart. Out of it spills the issues of life. *Be* these things that Jesus speaks of in the Beatitudes, not for yourself but for the good of others. *Be* these things because it puts you in a peaceful spirit that invites the Holy Spirit out of the wilderness and into your heart. *Be* these things, because when you do, you will learn an old forgotten language, the language of the heart. *Be* these things and most importantly, know your Shepherd's voice.

The Scripture

Matthew 5:1–15 "[1] When Jesus saw the crowds, He went up on the mountain; and when He was seated, His disciples came to Him. [2] Then He began to teach them, saying,

"³ Blessed [spiritually prosperous, happy, to be admired] are the poor in spirit [those devoid of spiritual arrogance, those who regard themselves as insignificant], for theirs is the kingdom of heaven [both now and forever].

"⁴ Blessed [forgiven, refreshed by God's grace] are those who mourn [over their sins and repent], for they will be comforted [when the burden of sin is lifted].

"⁵ Blessed [inwardly peaceful, spiritually secure, worthy of respect] are the gentle [the kind-hearted, the sweet-spirited, the self-controlled], for they will inherit the earth.

"⁶ Blessed [joyful, nourished by God's goodness] are those who hunger and thirst for righteousness [those who actively seek right standing with God], for they will be [completely] satisfied.

"⁷ Blessed [content, sheltered by God's promises] are the merciful, for they will receive mercy.

"⁸ Blessed [anticipating God's presence, spiritually mature] are the pure in heart [those with integrity, moral courage, and godly character], for they will see God.

"⁹ Blessed [spiritually calm with life-joy in God's favor] are the makers and maintainers of peace, for they will [express His character and] be called the sons of God.

"¹⁰ Blessed [comforted by inner peace and God's love] are those who are persecuted for doing that which is morally right, for theirs is the kingdom of heaven [both now and forever].

"¹¹ Blessed [morally courageous and spiritually alive with life-joy in God's goodness] are you when people insult you and persecute you, and falsely say all kinds of evil things against you because of [your association with] Me.

"12 Be glad and exceedingly joyful, for your reward in heaven is great [absolutely inexhaustible]; for in this same way they persecuted the prophets who were before you.

"13 You are the salt of the earth; but if the salt has lost its taste (purpose), how can it be made salty? It is no longer good for anything, but to be thrown out and walked on by people [when the walkways are wet and slippery].

"14 You are the light of [Christ to] the world. A city set on a hill cannot be hidden;

"15 nor does anyone light a lamp and put it under a basket, but on a lampstand, and it gives light to all who are in the house.

"16 Let your light shine before men in such a way that they may see your good deeds and moral excellence, and [recognize and honor and] glorify your Father who is in heaven."

Matthew 6:19–24 "19 Do not store up for yourselves [material] treasures on earth, where moth and rust destroy, and where thieves break in and steal. 20 But store up for yourselves treasures in heaven, where neither moth nor rust destroys, and where thieves do not break in and steal; 21 for where your treasure is, there your heart [your wishes, your desires; that on which your life centers] will be also.

"22 The eye is the lamp of the body; so if your eye is clear [spiritually perceptive], your whole body will be full of light [benefiting from God's precepts]. 23 But if your eye is bad [spiritually blind], your whole body will be full of darkness [devoid of God's precepts]. So if the [very] light inside you [your inner self, your heart, your conscience] is darkness, how great and terrible is that darkness!

"24 No one can serve two masters; for either he will hate the one and love the other, or he will be devoted to the one and despise the other. You cannot serve God and mammon [money, possessions, fame, status, or whatever is valued more than the Lord]."

Matthew 25:31–46 "31 But when the Son of Man comes in His glory and majesty and all the angels with Him, then He will sit on the throne of His glory. 32 All the nations will be gathered before Him [for judgment]; and He will separate them from one another, as a shepherd separates his sheep from the goats; 33 and He will put the sheep on His right [the place of honor], and the goats on His left [the place of rejection].

"34 Then the King will say to those on His right, 'Come, you blessed of My Father [you favored of God, appointed to eternal salvation], inherit the kingdom prepared for you from the foundation of the world. 35 For I was hungry, and you gave Me something to eat; I was thirsty, and you gave Me something to drink; I was a stranger, and you invited Me in; 36 I was naked, and you clothed Me; I was sick, and you visited Me [with help and ministering care]; I was in prison, and you came to Me [ignoring personal danger].' 37 Then the righteous will answer Him, 'Lord, when did we see You hungry, and feed You, or thirsty, and give You something to drink? 38 And when did we see You as a stranger, and invite You in, or naked, and clothe You? 39 And when did we see You sick, or in prison, and come to You?' 40 The King will answer and say to them, 'I assure you and most solemnly say to you, to the extent that you did it for one of these brothers of Mine, even the least of them, you did it for Me.'

"41 Then He will say to those on His left, 'Leave Me, you cursed ones, into the eternal fire which has been prepared for the devil and his angels (demons); 42 for I was hungry, and you gave Me nothing to eat; I was thirsty, and you gave Me nothing to drink; 43 I was a stranger, and you did not invite Me in; naked, and you did not clothe Me; sick, and in prison, and you did not visit Me [with help and ministering care].' 44 Then they also [in their turn] will answer, 'Lord, when did we see You hungry, or thirsty, or as a stranger, or naked, or sick, or in prison, and did not minister to You?' 45 Then He will reply to them, 'I assure you and most solemnly say to you, to the extent that you did not do it for one of the least of these [my followers], you did not do it for Me.' 46 Then these [unbelieving people] will go away into eternal (unending) punishment, but those who are righteous and in right standing with God [will go, by His remarkable grace] into eternal (unending) life."

The Assignment

"Be" ing

Search back through the scripture and find ten things that Jesus tells us to "be." After you find them imagine what it feels like to "be" these things. What does it feel like for others to see you "be" these things?

1. "Be" _____
2. "Be" _____
3. "Be" _____
4. "Be" _____

5. "Be" _____

6. "Be" _____

7. "Be" _____

8. "Be" _____

9. "Be" _____

10. "Be" _____

The Application

Write Things Down

Start keeping a journal of all the things that come from your heart throughout the day. Writing things down is one of the easiest ways to show the Holy Spirit that you acknowledge Him, you hear Him, and, most importantly you are willing to physically show it. Writing down these "breaths" of the Holy Spirit will help you to know His voice. Know your Shepherd's voice and keep a journal of His whispers. Writing it down is a way to guarantee that you get to hold onto it. The better you are at identifying His voice, the stronger the wind of His breath. Write down thoughts, write down feelings and write down grocery lists. Write down anything that you want to hold on to. Don't worry, it is not going to be required that you ever go back and read it.

The Questions

1. How do you know the Shepherd's voice?

2. Does this mean there can be other voices?

3. What is needed for you to use a spiritual gift? Why?

4. In what ways does applying what is inside of you to what is outside of you lead to fulfillment? Why?

5. Does raising your sails require more vulnerability or sensitivity? Why?

Chapter 5

The Picture:

Sailing Through Life

Take time when learning how to navigate your vessel. Recognize the things that work for you as well as the things that work against you. Even in Homer's poem, *The Odyssey*, Odysseus was warned of the challenges on his journey. Look out for yours. Agape for others will move you in directions and ways that you never thought possible. Learn to master yourself exactly as you find yourself today. Apply your gifts as you go. In keeping with our sailboat analogy, learn to master your craft in the harbor before you take it out into the ocean. Then, once mastered, come back for Level 2.

Agape (Ancient Greek: ἀγάπη, *agápē*) is "love: the highest form of love, charity; the love of God for man and of man for God."[1] Not to be confused with "phileo" - brotherly love - agápē embraces a universal, unconditional love that transcends, that serves regardless of circumstances.

—Wikipedia

The Story

Now it is time to set sail. You need to build momentum. Do this by winning small victories within your day. Get yourself moving before you venture out to take on anything else. Do this by daily managing little things—the things that are within your control. Focus on these things first, and then build enough momentum to win the big things. The best way to show God that you can handle more of something is by properly handling what you currently have.

Author John Maxwell puts it best: *"Get Good First."* Before you take off and challenge the world and all of its changing currents and winds, start close to home. Start with situations and hurdles you need to overcome daily. Master these first, humbly build some speed, and God will send more situations your way.

Once I realized that I naturally helped people and that I enjoyed presenting to people, I was able to apply this strategy to everything I faced. I did not have to go looking for any opportunities to apply my gifts. I found plenty of situations in my everyday life where I was able to practice—to get good.

I was consulting mostly in sales at the time, and discovered very quickly that I could help my clients to build a better business, just by being me. By applying my best self I would add value to their operation and they in turn would pay me for this added value. I found ways to serve in my local church that let me put my gifts to use. No longer did I focus on anyone else's skillset. No longer did I compare myself to anyone else. I was completely focused on applying my best self to the situations that were coming my way. I was efficient with my attention and focus.

I don't want it to sound like I just passively took a back seat to life, as it swirled on about me. That was not the case. I am a planner. I have my entire week planned out. God knows that. Every night I lift up my plan to Him. Every morning I trust that He knows what I need for the day. If things do not go according to the plan, <u>I trust it is because He came up with a better plan for me.</u> *I plan the weeks but I receive the day.* There is a difference.

The final obstacle for me before setting sail was that I had to overcome the thought that I had to be perfect before God could use me. I had to believe that there was something inside me—right here, right now—that was of value to other people.

It helped when I realized God had been using me for a lot longer than I had been aware of. His use of us is never reliant on our own awareness, thank goodness. But it is a lot more fun to team up with Him, so that you can see Him working through you. Plus, moving from a place of self-reliance to a place of God-reliance makes life a lot easier.

One last thing before I let you take off—and this is pretty big. It is imperative that you learn the difference between the voice(s) that you hear in your head and the one you hear in your heart. Trust the voice that is pure and from a place of love. Ask the others where they are coming from—because they will tell you.

Discerning God's voice can be tough at first. God's voice was always low and peaceful and always from a place of love—not just love for me, but for those whom I was a service to. You see, this whole thing is a *through* process, not a *to* process. It is all so that God can move through you as His hands and feet. All that you have uncovered, all that you have learned during this process is for the benefit of others. This is where true joy lies and this is where true peace is. True joy and peace comes from the benefit of others. This is fulfillment.

When you free yourself from the securities of this world and begin to rest in the arms of God, you will find peace. It will take intention, but it is well worth it. There are forces that you must grow beyond for a fuller expression of yourself. These forces want nothing more than to stop you from sharing with the physical world what is hidden inside of you. Stopping you from stepping into the life that you were meant to live. Now you have a reminder. Every time you see i² you will be reminded that fulfillment is on your doorstep. You just have to grab it, intentionally.

Here we are, each one of us on our individual boat ready to set sail. We have identified some parts of our boat that need some work. We have identified the anchors that must be lifted—none of which will stop us from raising our sails. Once our sails are raised, we will be lifted by the winds of the Spirit as we navigate the currents of life. Embark!

The Scripture

Isaiah 40:31 "But those who wait for the Lord [who expect, look for, and hope in Him] will gain new strength and renew their power; they will lift up their wings [and rise up close to God] like eagles [rising toward the sun]; they will run and not become weary, they will walk and not grow tired."

Romans 12:1–21 "¹² Therefore I urge you, brothers and sisters, by the mercies of God, to present your bodies [dedicating all of yourselves, set apart] as a living sacrifice, holy and well-pleasing to God, which is your rational (logical, intelligent) act of worship. ² And do not be conformed to this world [any longer with its superficial values and customs], but be transformed and progressively changed [as you mature spiritually] by the renewing of your mind [focusing on godly values and ethical attitudes], so that you may prove [for yourselves] what the will of God is, that which is good and acceptable and perfect [in His plan and purpose for you].

"³ For by the grace [of God] given to me I say to everyone of you not to think more highly of himself [and of his importance and ability] than he ought to think; but to think so as to have sound judgment, as God has apportioned to each a degree of faith [and a purpose designed for service]. [4] For just as in one [physical] body we have many parts, and these parts do not all have the same function or special use, [5] so we, who are many, are [nevertheless just] one body in Christ, and individually [we are] parts one of another [mutually dependent on each other]. [6] Since we have gifts that differ according to the grace given to us, each of us is to use them accordingly: if [someone has the gift of] prophecy, [let him speak a new message from God to His people] in proportion to the faith possessed; [7] if service, in the act of serving; or he who teaches, in the act of teaching; [8] or he who encourages, in the act of encouragement; he who gives, with generosity; he who leads, with diligence; he who shows mercy [in caring for others], with cheerfulness.

"[9] Love is to be sincere and active [the real thing—without guile and hypocrisy]. Hate what is evil [detest all ungodliness, do not tolerate wickedness]; hold on tightly to what is good. [10] Be devoted to one another with [authentic] brotherly affection [as members of one family], give preference to one another in honor; [11] never lagging behind in diligence; aglow in the Spirit, enthusiastically serving the Lord; [12] constantly rejoicing in hope [because of our confidence in Christ], steadfast and patient in distress, devoted to prayer [continually seeking wisdom, guidance, and strength], [13] contributing to the needs of God's people, pursuing [the practice of] hospitality.

"[14] Bless those who persecute you [who cause you harm or hardship]; bless and do not curse [them]. [15] Rejoice with those who rejoice [sharing others' joy], and weep with those who weep [sharing others' grief]. ¹⁶ Live in harmony with one another; do not be haughty [conceited, self-important, exclusive], but associate with humble people [those with a realistic self-view]. Do not overestimate yourself. ¹⁷ Never repay anyone evil for evil. Take thought for what is right and gracious and proper in the sight of everyone. ¹⁸ If possible, as far as it depends on you, live at peace with everyone. ¹⁹ Beloved, never avenge yourselves, but leave the way open for God's wrath [and His judicial righteousness]; for it is written [in Scripture], 'Vengeance is Mine, I will repay,' says the Lord. '²⁰ But if your enemy is hungry, feed him; if he is thirsty, give him a drink; for by doing this you will heap burning coals on his head.' ²¹ Do not be overcome and conquered by evil, but overcome evil with good."

Ephesians 6:10–20 "¹⁰ In conclusion, be strong in the Lord [draw your strength from Him and be empowered through your union with Him] and in the power of His [boundless] might. ¹¹ Put on the full armor of God [for His precepts are like the splendid armor of a heavily-armed soldier], so that you may be able to [successfully] stand up against all the schemes and the strategies and the deceits of the devil. ¹² For our struggle is not against flesh and blood [contending only with physical opponents], but against the rulers, against the powers, against the world forces of this [present] darkness, against the spiritual forces of wickedness in the heavenly (supernatural) places. ¹³ Therefore, put on the complete armor of God, so that you will be able to [successfully] resist and stand your ground in the evil day [of danger], and having done everything [that the crisis demands], to stand firm [in your place, fully prepared, immovable, victorious].

[14] So stand firm and hold your ground, having tightened the wide band of truth (personal integrity, moral courage) around your waist and having put on the breastplate of righteousness (an upright heart), [15] and having strapped on your feet the gospel of peace in preparation [to face the enemy with firm-footed stability and the readiness produced by the good news]. [16] Above all, lift up the [protective] shield of faith with which you can extinguish all the flaming arrows of the evil one. [17] And take the helmet of salvation, and the sword of the Spirit, which is the Word of God.

"[18] With all prayer and petition pray [with specific requests] at all times [on every occasion and in every season] in the Spirit, and with this in view, stay alert with all perseverance and petition [interceding in prayer] for all God's people. [19] And pray for me, that words may be given to me when I open my mouth, to proclaim boldly the mystery of the good news [of salvation], [20] for which I am an ambassador in chains. And pray that in proclaiming it I may speak boldly and courageously, as I should."

The Assignment:

SWOT

This is your SWOT Analysis. Fill out the graph following the instructions below:

○ Strengths: These are three of your strongest spiritual gifts.

○ Weaknesses: Three traits you have learned about yourself that make using these gifts difficult by taking you out of the present moment.

○ Opportunities: Three scenarios where you may use these gifts. If you are not sure, ask God. Then wait on Him to show you.

○ Threats: Three external factors that could prevent you from using these gifts. These are often your anchors.

By graphing your SWOT analysis, you now have a map legend for your life. You now know what areas to steer clear of, and which areas will reward you. Navigate wisely!

	Helpful	Harmful
I n t e r n a l	Strengths	Weaknesses
E x t e r n a l	Opportunities	Threats

The Application

Pull out your weekly calendar. Until you get momentum built, this is how I want you to use it. Ask yourself, "did I handle the situations that God sent me the way He intended?" This is not something anyone else can answer for you. It is between you and God. He sent you a situation or two today and expected you to use one or more of the gifts that He put inside you. Without judging your wins and losses as good or bad, I want you to record them—a green ✔ for yes, a red ✗ for no. Win your week by winning your days. When you start winning your weeks, start tracking months!

The Questions

1. What does it mean to wait on the Lord? Why is this important when using your Spiritual Gifts?

2. How do you build momentum? In what areas of your life is it wise to build momentum?

3. What areas of your life can you apply your strengths to right now? What is the best way to get started?

4. Is one area of you (mind, body and spirit) more important? Why?

5. In what ways can you steer clear of your *threats* and *weaknesses*?

Congratulations! Level 1 complete! Celebrate, but not for too long. The GI Joes were right in saying, "Knowing is half the battle." The true measure of growth is not determined by what you know; it's revealed in the self-control you show. Regardless, choosing to move beyond a state of unconsciousness and into a state of awareness is going to change your life. Fasten your seat belt, because there is no such thing as growing backwards, and we have a long way to grow!

COMING SOON

Level 2: *A Guide to Growing*
Level 3: *Survival Skills*
Level 4: *Rules and Regulations*
Level 5: *Unlocking a Humble Heart*

See you on the next level!
Thank you

About the Author

John Matthew Kilpatrick was born in Charleston, South Carolina, and raised in Birmingham, Alabama. John Matthew is the father of one son, Mason, and husband to his wife, Tiffany. Matthew is a small business consultant, life coach, and public speaker. His philosophy in business and life coaching is effectiveness and efficiency through leadership development.

Printed in the United States
By Bookmasters